Tree

A TEMPLAR BOOK
First published in the UK in 2010 by Templar Publishing,
an imprint of The Templar Company Limited,
The Granary, North Street, Dorking, Surrey RH4 1DN
www.templarco.co.uk

Conceived and produced by Weldon Owen Pty Ltd
59-61 Victoria Street, McMahons Point
Sydney, NSW 2060, Australia

BONNIER BOOKS
Group Publisher John Owen

WELDON OWEN PTY LTD
Chief Executive Officer Sheena Coupe
Creative Director Sue Burk
Art Manager Trucie Henderson

Senior Vice President, International Sales Stuart Laurence
Sales Manager: United States Ellen Towell
Vice President, Sales: Asia and Latin America Dawn L. Owen
Administration Manager, International Sales Kristine Ravn
Production Manager Todd Rechner
Production Coordinators Lisa Conway, Mike Crowton
Production Assistant Nathan Grice

Concept Design Arthur Brown/Cooling Brown
Project Editor Lesley McFadzean
Designer Karen Sagovac
Picture Researcher Joanna Collard

Illustrators The Art Agency (Rob Davis, Geraint Ford), Peter Bull
Art Studio, Contact Jupiter (Yvan Meunier), KJA-artists (Roger
Stewart), James McKinnon

ISBN 978-1-84877-185-7

Printed by Toppan Leefung Printing Limited
Manufactured in China

10 9 8 7 6 5 4 3 2 1

The paper used in the manufacture of this book is sourced
from wood grown in sustainable forests. It complies with the
Environmental Management System Standard ISO 14001:2004

A WELDON OWEN PRODUCTION

About the Author
David Burnie worked as a biologist and nature reserve ranger
before starting a career as a writer specialising in wildlife
and the environment. He has written or contributed to more
than a hundred books, ranging from field guides to major
encyclopedias on birds, mammals, ocean life and dinosaurs.
Several of his books have won scientific awards. He has studied
forests and their wildlife around the world, from the Scottish
Highlands to Southeast Asia and Costa Rica. He lives and
works in France.

INFINITY

Tree

FROM SEED TO MIGHTY FOREST

DAVID BURNIE

templar publishing

Contents

WHAT IS A
TREE?

Trees are easy to recognise because they tower above most other plants. Unlike other plants, they are made of wood – one of the toughest building materials in the living world. Singly, or in forests, trees are a vital part of Earth's ecosystem. They provide homes for many creatures, from tiny insects to large mammals. By taking in carbon dioxide and giving out oxygen, they are critical to the circulation of the atmosphere and help to keep the planet healthy. And, of course, we use their wood and other products in all kinds of ways.

Summary

Summer
Once the flowers have been pollinated, they start to form fruit. The fruit turns red when it is ripe, showing birds that it is ready to eat. Birds carry off the fruit, helping to spread the tree's seeds.

When the buds burst, the leaves are often a dark colour, turning bright green as they expand.

TYPES OF TREE

SPORE-BEARING TREES

SEED-BEARING TREES

Cycads

Ginkgo

Conifers

Angiosperms
(broadleaved trees)

Primitive angiosperms

Monocots

Dicots

What kind of tree?
There are two types of tree: spore-bearing trees, such as tree ferns; and seed-bearing trees, such as cycads, ginkgoes, conifers and angiosperms. Angiosperms, such as primitive angiosperms, monocots and dicots, have flowers, are broad-leaved and are seed-bearing. Dicots make up the biggest group of flowering trees in the world today.

Brightly coloured flowers attract pollinating insects.

Spring
As the days lengthen in spring, the cherry tree emerges from its winter sleep. Its buds swell, then burst, and its young leaves open up in the warm sunshine. The flowers follow soon after.

Autumn

As the days shorten, the tree prepares to shed its leaves. It breaks down some of the chemicals the leaves contain, which makes them change into their autumn colours. Shortly after this happens, the leaves begin to fall.

Leaves fall when a corky layer seals off their stalks.

CHANGING WITH THE SEASONS

Some trees are evergreen, which means that they keep their leaves all year round. But in places with long winters, broadleaved trees are often deciduous, dropping all their leaves before the cold weather starts. When spring arrives, they suddenly come back to life, as their buds burst and their new leaves begin to grow. Some of these trees – including cherry trees – create a spectacular display of flowers at this time of year.

Buds protect next year's shoots.

Bark stops twigs and branches from drying out.

TREE TIMELINE

SILURIAN PERIOD
(445–415 million years ago)
Cooksonia – earliest land plant, about 5 centimetres (2 in) high.

CARBONIFEROUS PERIOD
(360–300 million years ago)
Lepidodendron – tree-like giant clubmoss, up to 30 metres (98 ft) high; fossilised remains formed coal.

TRIASSIC PERIOD
(250–200 million years ago)
Araucaria (monkey puzzles/ Chile pines) – widespread conifers during the dinosaur age, still alive today.

CRETACEOUS PERIOD
(145–65 million years ago)
Magnolia – among the first flowering trees, still alive today.

Winter

In winter, the tree looks dead but it is still very much alive. It hardens the wood that it grew during the summer and shuts down its root tips to protect them from frost. Without its leaves, the tree can withstand temperatures lower than a deep freeze.

In winter, sugary sap is stored in the tree's roots.

TREE FERNS

TREE FERNS have existed for more than 300 million years, which makes them among the most ancient group of plants on Earth. Instead of growing seeds, they spread by growing dust-like specks called "spores". Tree ferns have fibrous trunks, rather than true wood, and are usually less than 15 metres (49 ft) high. Most tree ferns live in damp, shaded habitats, where they are protected from bright sunlight and strong winds.

UNCURLING *Tree ferns have feathery leaves, known as fronds. They grow by uncurling toward their tips.*

SPORE FACTORIES *Most tree ferns make their spores on the underside of their fronds. The spores drift away on the wind.*

FERN FOREST *Tree ferns are common in the southern hemisphere. These ones are growing in a rainforest in New Zealand.*

VITAL
ROOTS

Like tall buildings, trees need solid foundations to keep them in place. They also need to collect water and nutrients from the soil. Both these tasks are carried out by roots, which fan out through the ground. Roots grow in step with the rest of the tree. At first, they are small, delicate and very easy to break. But, by the time a tree reaches maturity, its biggest roots are as strong as a ship's cables, helping it to ride out storms. Laid end to end, a tree's entire root system may be thousands of kilometres long.

Turning into trunks

Banyan trees grow roots that hang down in the air. When these roots reach the ground, they turn into extra trunks. Some of the oldest banyan trees have over a hundred trunks that cover an area bigger than a tennis court.

SURVIVING IN SWAMPS

TREES LIVE in many different habitats, including areas that flood for part of the year. Only a few kinds of trees can survive being in water all year round because waterlogged ground makes a bad anchorage. Also, water contains less oxygen than soil, which makes it hard for roots to grow. To get around this problem, swamp-dwelling trees have specialised roots that prop them up and collect oxygen from the air.

SWAMP CYPRESSES *These grow in the southern USA. They have buttress roots and knobbly "knees" (pneumatophores) just above the water's surface.*

MANGROVES *In warm parts of the world, mangroves grow along shallow coasts. Prop roots anchor them in the tidal mud.*

Giant anteater

Leaf-cutter ants

Amazon
hog-nosed
pit viper

Giant centipede

Leaf litter is the
carpet of dead
leaves on the
forest floor.

Humus contains
small pieces of
dead leaves and
particles of
rotting wood.

Slice through the soil

The ground beneath a forest
has four different layers:
leaf litter, humus, topsoil
and bedrock. In tropical
rainforests, the top three
layers are often thin, so
tree roots stay close to the
surface, instead of growing
further down.

Topsoil contains
humus mixed
with particles
of bedrock.

Bedrock is the
deepest layer,
with only a few
living things.

Digging deep

In temperate forests, the cooler
climate means that dead leaves
and wood take longer to rot. As
a result, the soil is often richer
than in tropical rainforests and
tree roots grow deeper down.

BENEFICIAL BUGS

TREES DO NOT NEED FOOD but they do need simple substances called nutrients, which they collect with their roots. Most plant nutrients originally come from soil and rock but one of the most important – nitrogen – comes from the atmosphere. Strangely, trees cannot gather nitrogen from the air. Instead, they rely on soil bacteria to collect it. These "nitrogen-fixing" bacteria then turn it into a form that roots can absorb.

NODULES
Some trees have special growths on their roots that shelter nitrogen-fixing bacteria.

INSIDE ROOTS

In warm weather, a big tree can suck up more than 1,000 litres (220 gal) of water a day. All this water travels from the soil and up a tree's roots. At the same time, roots carry sap in the other direction, giving root tips the energy they need to grow. This two-way transport works through special pipelines, which connect the roots with every other part of the tree.

Roots revealed
Roots contain two different kinds of pipelines: xylem (pronounced *zy-lem*) and phloem (*flo-em*). Xylem carries water, while phloem carries sap. Each root absorbs water through thousands of microscopic hairs, which look like a fuzzy beard.

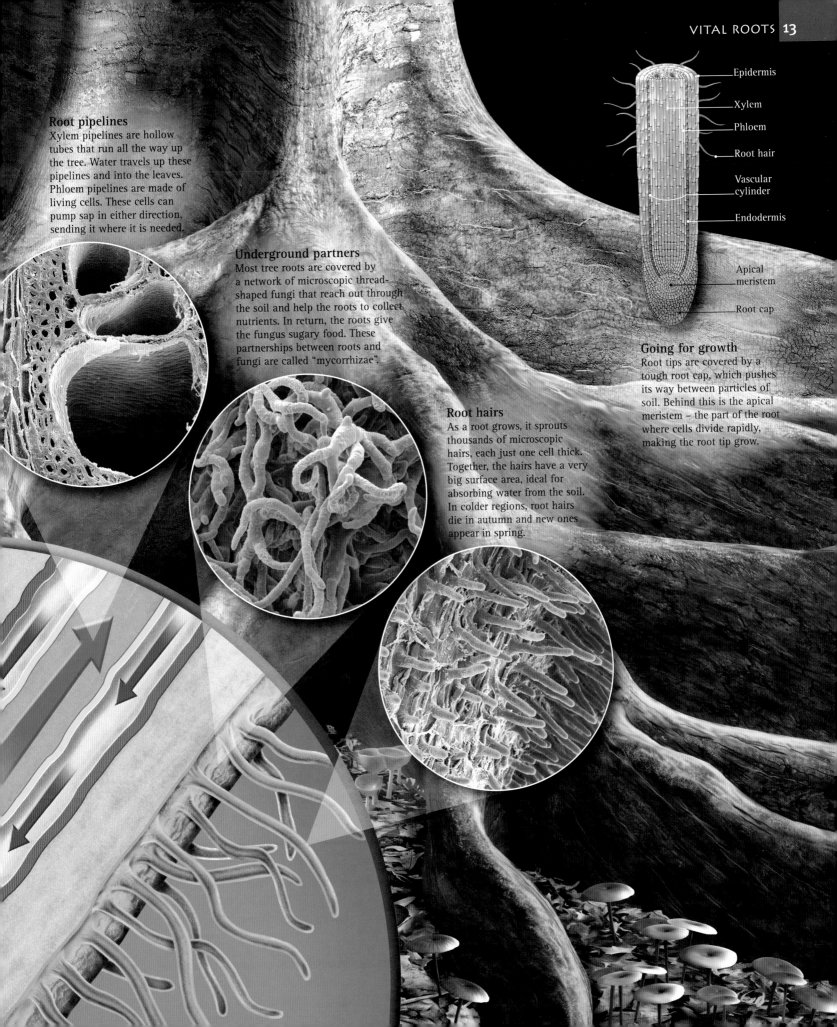

Epidermis

Xylem

Phloem

Root hair

Vascular cylinder

Endodermis

Apical meristem

Root cap

Root pipelines

Xylem pipelines are hollow tubes that run all the way up the tree. Water travels up these pipelines and into the leaves. Phloem pipelines are made of living cells. These cells can pump sap in either direction, sending it where it is needed.

Underground partners

Most tree roots are covered by a network of microscopic thread-shaped fungi that reach out through the soil and help the roots to collect nutrients. In return, the roots give the fungus sugary food. These partnerships between roots and fungi are called "mycorrhizae".

Going for growth

Root tips are covered by a tough root cap, which pushes its way between particles of soil. Behind this is the apical meristem – the part of the root where cells divide rapidly, making the root tip grow.

Root hairs

As a root grows, it sprouts thousands of microscopic hairs, each just one cell thick. Together, the hairs have a very big surface area, ideal for absorbing water from the soil. In colder regions, root hairs die in autumn and new ones appear in spring.

Head for hammering

Woodpeckers have especially strong skulls to absorb the impact as they hammer into tree bark with their tough beaks. Once the bark is smashed, they find wood-boring grubs with their long, spiny tongues.

TYPES OF BARK

When identifying trees, many people think first of the leaves, flowers and fruits. But looking at different types of bark is another tool to use. Bark varies from smooth to furrowed, from thorny to coloured, from oozing to stringy.

The rainbow eucalyptus tree has amazing multicoloured bark.

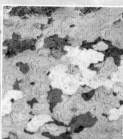

The stringybark gum sheds its old bark in long strips.

Plane trees have scaly bark

Pine trees ooze sticky resin if they are injured.

The honeylocust has spiny thorns all over its bark.

Black walnut bark is dark

BARK AND
TRUNK

Soaring high into the air, the trunk is the biggest and strongest part of any tree. Its strength is vital because it shoulders the tremendous weight of branches and leaves, as well as the water and sap that the tree needs to grow. Tree trunks do this by having lots of layers, which work in quite different ways. The hardest layer is the heartwood, which is deep inside the trunk. The busiest layer is just under the bark because this is where the trunk grows. The bark itself is like a tough jacket, keeping pests and diseases at bay.

A good grip

Squirrels usually feed on seeds, berries or nuts, but in spring the supply runs out. That's when they gnaw on trees to get to the sugar-rich sapwood beneath the bark. Their sharp, curved claws help them to grasp onto the tree trunk.

Bark stripped by squirrels takes time to recover.

Stepping up

Palm trees do not have true bark and their trunks do not get thicker as they grow. They often have rough scars left behind by falling leaves. These scars make useful steps for climbing up the tree.

Tree fern trunks

Tree ferns do not have real wood and their trunks feel stringy and soft. They are held up by leaf-stalks, packed together to make a pole. This kind of trunk is not very strong, which is why tree ferns cannot grow very high.

Cross-section of a tree-fern trunk

RUBBER TREE

I F A TROPICAL rubber tree is injured, it will ooze sap from its bark, called latex. This latex is produced in latex vessels in the phloem layer underneath the bark. Latex is collected from the tree in a process known as rubber tapping. Cuts made in the bark make the milky-white sticky fluid flow out. This juice, caught in a vessel, can then be dried and made into rubber.

A KIND CUT *Diagonal cuts are made in the bark just deep enough to harvest the latex without harming the tree's growth.*

MADE OF RUBBER *There are hundreds of products which start life with the rubber tree – including bicycle tyres.*

Heartwood is at the centre of the trunk. It is hard, dark and very strong.

Growth rings

In most parts of the world, trees grow quickly in spring and early summer then stop growing before the winter sets in. Each spurt of growth adds a ring of new wood just beneath the bark. Adding up these rings shows how old a tree is.

A wide ring shows rapid growth.

Heartwood, which consists of dead cells, is the oldest part of the tree.

Sapwood contains vessel-like xylem cells that carry water upward from the roots.

Inside a tree trunk

No two tree trunks are exactly alike but most have five different layers, wrapped around a heartwood core. Heartwood and sapwood give the trunk its strength, while a thin layer called the vascular cambium makes the trunk grow.

The outer bark is made of dead cells. It protects the trunk from pests and temperature extremes.

The inner bark has cells that produce new bark as the trunk expands.

Phloem is the layer in which sap travels around the tree.

Vascular cambium is the layer with cells that divide to make the trunk thicker.

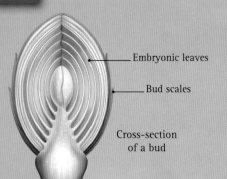

Embryonic leaves

Bud scales

Cross-section of a bud

GOING FOR GROWTH

The horse chestnut has extra-large buds, which are covered with a sticky resin. In spring, when they swell up and burst open, the tree starts a spectacular surge of growth. During the summer, the new twigs harden and the next set of buds starts to form. By the autumn, the tree is ready to shut down again for its winter sleep.

Young leaves are protected from the wind by silky fur.

Terminal buds, at the ends of twigs, are bigger than the lateral ones along the sides.

1 The bud's scales overlap like tiles on a roof. This seals in moisture and protects the embryo shoot from cold winds. Sticky resin cements them together and makes it harder for plant-eating insects to get inside.

Scales fold back and dry out.

TWIGS AND

BUDS

Branches can weigh many tonnes but even the biggest start life as slender twigs. In warm parts of the world, twigs have leaves all year round but, in colder places, twigs can be bare for many months each year. Most broadleaved trees prepare for winter by growing buds. Buds are miniature shoots, sealed up from the wind and frost outside. During the winter, they stay shut tight and show no signs of life. But in spring, as the days get longer, they gradually start to swell. Suddenly, millions of buds burst, as if triggered by a starter's gun.

Lateral buds develop only if the terminal bud is broken off.

2 In spring, chemicals in the tree's sap make the bud start growing. It gradually swells and then its scales fold back, revealing the young shoot inside. Powered by the spring sunshine, the shoot grows at up to 2.5 centimetres (1 in) a day.

Prime location
Many trees grow their buds in leaf axils. An axil is the narrow space between a leaf stalk and a twig. In autumn, when the leaves fall, each bud is left with the room that it needs to grow.

Scar left by terminal bud

Twig produced during previous year's growth

Scar left by terminal bud

Lenticels on surface of twig

Scar left by leaf from the previous year

Vapourer moth caterpillar

Bird and caterpillar
Many insects, such as moths, time the laying of their eggs so that their larvae – caterpillars – can take advantage of the newly emerged leaves. In turn, many birds lay their eggs so that their young can feast on the caterpillars.

Great tit

Bursting into bloom
It is not only leaves that form inside buds. Many trees produce embryo flowers in the autumn, and then pack them away inside buds until the following spring.

The flowerhead contains dozens of separate flowers, attached to an upright stalk.

3 As the leaves expand, the flowerhead emerges from the centre of the shoot. Within three or four weeks, the leaves will be as wide as a dinner plate and the flowers will form a majestic spire up to 30 centimetres (12 in) high.

WINTER COVER UP

JUST LIKE we wear different, weatherproof clothes in winter, buds too have many different kinds of weatherproof scales. In cold parts of the world, these scales can keep buds alive even when the temperature drops to –35ºC (–31ºF). Buds often contain their own antifreeze but scales also stop a bud from drying out – something that is much more dangerous than the cold alone.

STICKY COAT *Rowans and many other trees have resin-coated buds.*

FUR JACKET *Pussy willow buds have smooth scales and then develop furry catkins.*

BLACK BUDS *Ash trees have small buds with velvety jet-black scales.*

The leaf has five or seven leaflets, which spread out flat as they grow.

1 In the maple, the flower buds open before the leaves.

2 The lateral buds contain either male or female flowers.

3 When the flowers are open, the terminal bud begins to develop.

4 By the time the leaves emerge, the flowers are long gone.

Spiral leaves

Whorled leaves

LEAF SHAPES

Conifer needles are long and thin, while conifer scales are short and flat. Broadleaved trees have two overall leaf types. Simple leaves have a single blade but compound leaves are divided up into separate parts, called leaflets.

Conifer needles

Compound leaf

ARRANGEMENTS

Instead of growing at random, leaves are arranged in four main ways. Alternate leaves grow singly, while opposite leaves grow in pairs. Whorled leaves grow in rings and spiral leaves coil around the stem.

Opposite leaves

Simple leaf

Conifer scales

Leaf blade

Margin or leaf edge

Mid rib

Network of veins

Alternate leaf

DIFFERENT

LEAVES

From far away, trees can be difficult to tell apart. But if you get up close, you can find out more by looking at their leaves. Conifer leaves are often dark green and are shaped like needles or scales. They are usually evergreen, which means that they stay on the tree all year round. The leaves of broadleaved trees are flat, with countless different shapes and shades of green. Many of these leaves are deciduous, falling off before winter begins. During the autumn, they often colour up before they fall – a sign that cold weather is on its way.

Petiole or leaf stalk

Stipule

EAF MARGINS

ome broadleaved trees have
mooth-edged leaves. But many
aves have complicated margins
r edges, with deep notches or
ny teeth. These help them
 grow in different climates
nd to collect enough light.

Serrate or
toothed leaf

Dissected or
eeply cut leaf

Entire or
smooth-edged
leaf

Obtuse or
blunt-tipped
leaf

LEAF TIPS

A leaf's tip is like the trailing edge
of an aeroplane's wing. It has to cope
with turbulence from the wind and
it also channels rainwater off the leaf,
which helps the surface to stay clean.

Acuminate or
pointed leaf

Notched leaf

DEADLY DEFENCES

LEAVES ATTRACT lots of plant-eating animals, so
they need special defences to survive. Many are
protected by poisonous chemicals or by substances that
make them difficult to digest. In the tropics, some trees
have live-in ants. The ants swarm over the leaves if they
are touched, stinging any animal that they meet. The
New Zealand ongaonga is even more dangerous – its
leaves are armed with painful stings.

ONGAONGA *This
dangerous relative of
the stinging nettle
grows up to 5 metres
(16 ft) high.*

CHANGING COLOUR

The North American sugar maple is famous for its
beautiful autumn colours. Colours like these are
produced when the tree starts to break down chlorophyll,
the chemical that normally makes leaves green. Once the
chlorophyll has been broken down, other chemicals in
the leaf become visible, making it turn red, orange,
yellow and then brown, before it finally falls.

Outer membrane

Fluid

Thylakoid

Chlorophyll

Starch grain

POWER FROM THE SUN

As soon as dawn breaks, the tree starts to collect solar energy and photosynthesis can get underway. To make photosynthesis work, trees need just two main ingredients: water from the soil and carbon dioxide from the air. Sunlight helps to keep the water and carbon dioxide moving.

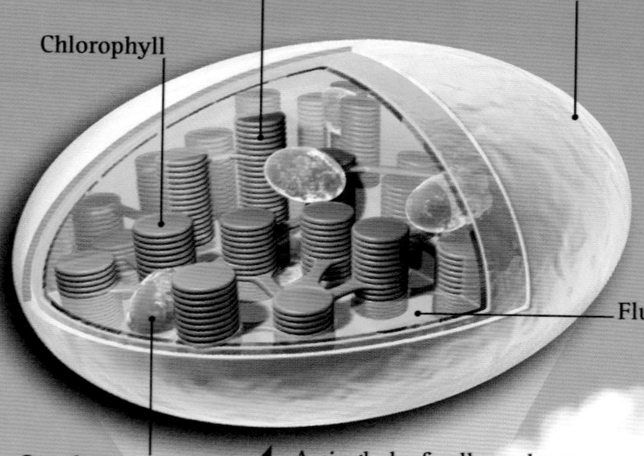

4 A single leaf cell can have thousands of chloroplasts. Each one contains flat sacs called thylakoids, arranged in upright stacks. On their surface, a green substance called chlorophyll receives solar energy and uses it to drive photosynthesis.

LIVING ON LIGHT

All living things need energy to work and to grow. We get our energy from food but trees get theirs in a very different way, by collecting light with their leaves. Their leaves work like solar panels, soaking up energy from the Sun. Inside each leaf, the energy that is in sunlight is used to make glucose – a sugar that works like a fuel. This process is called photosynthesis, which means "putting together by light". It is used by all green plants, and it is essential for us as well because it creates the food that we need to survive.

Sunlight

3 Leaves soak up the energy in sunshine. They use the energy to combine water with carbon dioxide from the air, producing glucose. This chemical reaction takes place in microscopic "work stations" called chloroplasts.

5 Photosynthesis creates two waste products – oxygen and water. They escape through the stomata into the air outside. Glucose, created by photosynthesis, is often converted into sucrose. Dissolved in sap, it is then moved out of the leaf to other parts of the tree.

Water vapour

Oxygen

Glucose uses

Plants use glucose in many ways. It powers their cells but it can also be made into many other substances. These include cellulose, a substance that makes cell walls, as well as sucrose, starch, resin and sap. This broken twig is oozing white sap.

2 The tree's leaves are covered with stomata, which are microscopic breathing pores. In sunny weather, the stomata open up wide, letting air in and out of the leaf. Most of the water evaporates through the stomata, sucking more water up the trunk. This is called transpiration.

Guard cell

Stoma (pore)

1 Water moves up the tree 24 hours a day but it travels fastest when the Sun begins to shine. In a large tree, water may travel more than 100 metres (330 ft) between the root tips and the highest leaves. The water is sucked upward in a non-stop stream.

KEY

- **WATER** MOVES UP THE TREE.
- **SUNLIGHT** PROVIDES ENERGY.
- **OXYGEN** COMES OUT OF THE LEAVES AS WASTE.
- **WATER VAPOUR** COMES OUT OF THE LEAVES AS WASTE.
- **GLUCOSE** MOVES AROUND THE TREE.

Soil story

As well as water, tree roots absorb natural minerals and nutrients from the soil. These are vital for the healthy growth of a tree. Without minerals, trees would not be able to make the chlorophyll that is essential for photosynthesis.

POLLEN AND
POLLINATION

U nlike animals, trees cannot move about, so they cannot get together to make seeds. Instead, they produce tiny pollen grains, which do the travelling for them. Pollen contains male cells, packaged up in specks smaller than grains of dust. If pollen lands on the right kind of flower, it fertilises the female cells and seeds can begin to form. Tree pollen makes its epic journey in different ways. Some trees shed clouds of pollen into the wind but others use visiting animals. To attract these visitors, they often grow eye-catching flowers.

Pollen factories
Conifers do not have flowers but they make pollen just like other trees. They do this with male cones. In pine trees, these are small and bright yellow. Male cones produce millions of pollen grains, which scatter in the wind.

ANCIENT FLOWERS
Magnolia trees have lived for millions of years, since the time of the dinosaurs. Their flowers are mainly pollinated by beetles, as bees did not even exist when they first bloomed. Magnolia carpels (female parts) are extra tough to avoid damage by crawling beetles. The following steps explain how a magnolia flower is pollinated, from the first visitor to fertilisation.

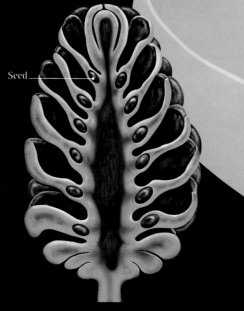

Seed

Anthers   Carpels

Home in a cone
To begin with, female cones are also small and soft but they turn hard as they grow. They are pollinated by the wind and their seeds develop deep inside, between the tough scales of the cone. When the seeds are ripe, the scales open up and the seeds flutter out.

1 Magnolia flowers have a set timetable. On day one, the flower's female parts (carpels) collect pollen from visiting insects. The carpels are arranged in a spiral, and each one has a chamber at its base called an ovary.

2 On day two, the male parts (anthers) open out, dabbing insects with pollen, which gets carried to other magnolia flowers. Once their work is done, the anthers fall away.

Birds
Bird-pollinated flowers
are often funnel-shaped
and red – a colour that
birds can see well.

ANIMAL VISITORS

IF A TREE has colourful flowers, you can be sure
that it is pollinated by animals. The commonest
pollinating animals are insects but, in some parts
of the world, trees are also pollinated by birds and
by bats. Insect-pollinated flowers are often small but
bird- and bat-pollinated flowers are bigger and stronger,
to avoid being damaged by flapping wings.

INSECTS *Bees and other insects*
are attracted to sweetly scented
flowers. They can smell them
from far away.

BATS *Many bat-pollinated flowers*
are white, so that they show up
at night. The flowers often have
a powerful smell.

Carpels

Attachment point
of anthers (shed
after pollination)

Ovary

Ovule

Pollen tube

Nucleus of male cell

Nucleus of female cell

3 If a pollen grain lands
on a carpel, it grows
a slender tube down
into the ovary to reach the
female ovule. The male cells
then travel down the tube
so that the ovule's female
nuclei can be fertilised, and
a new seed can form.

ALL ABOUT
SEEDS

For trees, the most important part of life is right at the beginning, when they are tucked up inside seeds. Seeds are tough and are specially designed to travel, so that young saplings can find the space that they need to grow. Some seeds move only a few metres before they put down roots. Others hitch a lift high over forests or across oceans, helped by animals, water or the wind. Conifers have bare seeds but broadleaved trees package their seeds inside fruits, which can be soft, or hard and dry.

FRUITS AND SEEDS

SOFT FRUITS
In these fruits, the seeds are surrounded by a fleshy outer layer.

Inside out
A fig is a very unusual fruit, made by tiny, inward-growing flowers. Together, these flowers produce hundreds of seeds. Birds feast on figs and, when they perch, scatter the fig's seeds. Some figs – called stranglers – germinate from seeds scattered high up in other trees.

Down in one
Apple seeds, or pips, grow inside juicy fruits. In the wild, they are often eaten by thrushes and other birds. The birds digest the apple's flesh but the seeds pass through their bodies, unharmed and ready to germinate.

Special protection
A peach has a single seed, called a stone, surrounded by sweet-tasting flesh. Stones have a skin that feels like wood and they are so hard that very few animals can crack them open. This gives the seed the best chance of survival.

FRUITS WITH NUTS
Nuts are seeds with a tough outer shell. The fruit around them can be hard as well, protecting them from damage.

Specially planted
Brazil nuts grow inside small, coconut-like fruits. When a fruit falls, its seeds are often eaten by mammals called agoutis, which bury any leftover seeds. These seeds germinate into new trees.

Ready for eating
When a nutmeg is ripe, it splits open, revealing a lacy covering called an aril. Its bright red colour attracts birds that swallow the nutmeg whole. Later, they cough up the seed.

Prickly protection
The sweet chestnut has prickly fruit to protect its seeds. When the seeds are ripe, the fruit falls and splits open. The nuts are scattered by animals, including birds, squirrels and wild boar.

SEEDS THAT TRAVEL

IN THE WORLD OF TREES, the greatest travellers glide on the wind or drift on the high seas. Gliding seeds often have wings or feathery hairs. Drifting seeds have buoyant husks and tough shells that protect them when they get washed up on the shore. Coconuts have been found as far north as Norway – thousands of kilometres away from their natural habitat.

SAFELY ASHORE *After weeks at sea, this coconut has been washed up on a beach. It must take root quickly to avoid being washed away.*

HELICOPTER SEEDS *Maple seeds grow in pairs and have papery wings. When the seeds fall, they spin through the air like helicopters.*

TREES, BIRDS AND SEEDS

A toco toucan flies over the forest with a meal gripped in its beak. Toucans help trees because they cough up seeds after they have digested their food. But birds aren't always this useful. Macaws and cockatoos crack open nuts with their powerful beaks and eat the seeds before they have a chance to germinate.

First true leaves

Coytledons (seed leaves)

Hypocotyl (stem)

Seed case splits open.

Radicle

From seed to sapling

As soon as conditions are just right, a seed will begin to grow – a process called germination. For this to happen, the seed needs water, warmth and oxygen. Here, we follow an apple seed's journey from seed to sapling.

1 The radicle (early root) pushes its way through the seed coat into the soil.

2 Roots develop. The hypocotyl (stem) begins to straighten and pulls the cotyledons (seed leaves) into the air.

3 The seed case has fallen off. The seed leaves begin to unfold, and the stem straightens further.

4 The first true leaves (which look like leaves on an adult tree) start to grow. The seed leaves will fall off eventually.

CHANGING SHAPES

SOME TREES CHANGE radically during their lifetime. The toothed lancewood, a tree from New Zealand, is almost unrecognisable as a sapling, with a different growth form and completely different leaves from the adult tree. During its 500-year lifetime, an English oak changes shape from a straggling sapling to a majestic giant. It grows outward as much as upward, so that its spread is often greater than its height.

A young oak sapling

A MATURE OAK TREE *in its prime, growing in open parkland*

SILHOUETTES AND
SHAPES

When animals grow up, they are almost always the same shape as their parents. Things aren't quite so simple in the world of trees. That's because trees are shaped by their surroundings, as well as by the genes they inherit. For example, forest trees often grow tall and thin but, in the open, the trees spread out because they have more room. Trees also change shape as they grow older and they can be sculpted by animals that eat them. In Africa's grassy plains, flat-topped thorn trees are shaped by the world's tallest leaf eater – the giraffe.

Flag trees
On coasts and other exposed places, trees can be sculpted by the wind. Branches on the side facing the prevailing wind are killed off; those on the opposite side seem to stream out, like a flag flying from a mast.

TREE SHAPES

Although they can be shaped by weather and grazing animals, trees each have a basic pattern that is created by the way they grow and branch, and is adapted to the conditions in which they live. Some have evolved to cope with drought or salt winds; others to survive snow and freezing temperatures.

Mop-headed trees
Unlike woody trees, palms have a single bud at the crown, from which the leaves are produced. As the leaves die and are shed, they leave behind leaf scars on the fibrous trunk.

Round trees
Trees that grow out in the open are often very different in shape from those that grow in woodland, where they have to compete for light. A solitary oak will form a large, round crown that takes full advantage of any sunlight.

Columnar trees
Some trees from hot, dry climates, such as the Lombardy poplar from Italy, grow as a narrow column. This means that at midday, when the sun is direct overhead, only the narrow circular crown is exposed to the full heat.

WILDLIFE OR WEATHER

Trees are shaped by many things. Each starts with a basic genetic blueprint, unique to its species. But the final shape of each individual tree is influenced by the soil it grows in, the weather it experiences and the effects of grazing animals. For instance, an African thorn tree battles against plant-eating mammals throughout its life, eventually outgrowing all of them except the giraffe. It is the long reach of the giraffe, 6 metres (19.5 ft) or more, that determines the final shape of the tree.

Flat-topped trees
Grazing by animals such as deer, goats and giraffes can remove all the lower branches within their reach. This often produces a tree with most of its leaves in a flat-topped crown.

Drooping trees
Although it is related to the oak and beech, the casuarina has greatly reduced leaves and looks more like a conifer. The thin, drooping branches and scale-like leaves make it very resistant to dry winds.

Triangular trees
Many conifers produce branches that continue to grow slowly over a period of several years. The lower branches are therefore longer than those towards the top, which are still growing. This makes a pyramid shape that sheds snow more easily in winter.

Umbrella trees
Some trees form a wide, thin crown, shaped very much like an umbrella. The large surface area captures the greatest amount of sunlight from the smallest number of leaves.

Grandfather and the sapling

THE STORY OF AN INDIAN BEAN TREE
A FAMILY TREE

For four generations, our backyard was home to a special tree. My great-grandfather planted it, way back in 1920, and it almost became one of the family. Great-grandpa must have known a few things about trees because it was great for shade in the summer but, unlike some garden trees, never got too big. And those flowers – wow! They say there's nothing quite like an Indian bean tree when it's in full bloom. The flowers have wavy-edged petals and they grow in clusters that look like giant helpings of ice cream. They are loaded with sugary nectar, which attracts bees, butterflies and even hummingbirds, all keen for a share of the feast. But these flying visitors have to be quick. The flowers don't last long and, when their petals drop off, they look like snow lying on the ground.

One of our oldest photos of the tree shows my grandfather standing next to it, at the age of about five or six. You wouldn't guess it but trees actually became a way of life to him because he worked in forestry research. We lived in Virginia and, when I was young, my grandfather would take me on hikes, stopping to look at trees along the way. Thanks to him, I found out that our family tree grows wild in the southeastern states of the USA. It is called the Indian bean tree after its pods, which split open to scatter its seeds. Its other names – the catalpa or catawba – were given to it by native Americans, long before Europeans arrived on the scene. And it's not the only catalpa species. There are nearly a dozen kinds of catalpa although "our" tree is the kind you're most likely to see.

"The flowers… grow in clusters that look like giant helpings of ice cream."

Trees take a while to find their feet and ours waited until the 1930s before really taking off. Back then, family photos were still in black and white, so you can see its long dark seed pods but not the beautiful lime-green colour of its leaves. By the time my dad came along, in the early 1950s, it was twice as high as the fence and had really thickened out. Dad may have been small but the tree wasn't a baby any more.

I grew up a few kilometres from my grandparents and their back garden was like a private playground for me and my friends. I was born in 1985, which means that our tree was then about 65 years old. Officially, I wasn't allowed to climb it but

Great-grandfather's diary

~ CATALPA ~
or Indian Bean Tree
(Catalpa bignonioides)

19 July 1920 Today I planted a catalpa tree in the garden to celebrate the birth of my son. This most attractive tree will give us shade and should live long enough for my grandsons and ... to enjoy.

Bean pods growing on the tree

Ripe bean pods

Me climbing the tree

My dad in 1958

I found out that it could easily stand my weight. I wasn't the only one that liked it – the local birds seemed to love its shade. Some of them nested in its branches, even though the catalpa is one of the last trees to come into leaf each year.

"...a split opened up in its bark, close to the ground."

Our tree also attracted other kinds of wildlife. One summer, the tree was infested by finger–sized caterpillars marked with thick black stripes. People around here call them "catalpa worms" but they are actually produced by the catalpa sphinx – a kind of hawkmoth that lives on catalpa trees. After munching through the leaves for about a month, the caterpillars climb down the trunk and turn into chrysalises underground. Months later, the chrysalises split open and a new generation of moths flies away to lay eggs on other catalpa trees.

Fortunately, our tree seemed none the worse after its insect attack. As the years came and went, it kept going strong. By the late 1990s, it was more than 75 years old, which in catalpa years is about middle age. It was in great shape, so we all expected it to be around in 2020, when it would have reached its centenary.

Unfortunately, nature decided otherwise. During a heatwave in the summer of 2007, a split opened up in its bark, close to the ground. The following year, there were more signs of trouble. Those wonderful green leaves weren't so green any more. On some of the branches, they turned yellow a few weeks after opening and soon dropped off. My grandfather – our resident tree expert – recognised the warning signs. Fungi had got through the break in the bark and infected the tree. Grandpa got my dad to saw off the affected branches and carry them away to be burned. That helped for a while but it couldn't stop the rot. The fungus eventually spread too far and, in 2009, our Indian bean tree had to come down.

We've all missed it since but grandpa isn't one for letting the grass grow under his feet. He's already deciding what to plant in its place.

Kai Daniel

Catalpa bark and flower

Blossom and leaves

TREES AS
HABITAT

From spring right through to autumn, the tulip tree teems with life. It's one of the tallest trees in the Appalachian forests of the eastern United States, and its leafy canopy is the top of a multi-storey habitat up to 45 metres (147 ft) high. Birds and mammals often use the tree as their base but for many insects it is a permanent home, stocked with nutritious food. These tiny tree dwellers are incredibly numerous and can damage even the tallest trees.

Safety in numbers
Intelligent and adaptable, blue jays find all kinds of food on and around tulip trees. They usually keep themselves to themselves but, if a predator comes too close, they will gang together to chase it away.

From egg to adult
Tiger swallowtails often lay their eggs on the leaves of tulip trees. Their caterpillars live on their own, inside silk tents that protect them from hungry birds. They spend the winter in a chrysalis and turn into adult butterflies the following spring.

Night flight
During the day, the northern flying squirrel sleeps in a tree hole. It emerges after dark, gliding between trees on "wings" made of flaps of stretched skin. Flying squirrels are mostly vegetarian – fungi top the list of their favourite foods.

UNWELCOME GUESTS

DESPITE THEIR SMALL SIZE, insects have big appetites and they can cause lasting damage to trees. Most insects are very particular about the food they eat and cannot live on anything else. Some bore their way through wood or chew through leaves. Others live entirely on sap, sucking it up through mouth parts that work like tiny syringes.

TULIP TREE SCALE
Female scale insects feed on sap. They have humped bodies and cannot move.

BORER *This moth's wood-boring caterpillars eat the tree's sapwood, allowing fungi to get in.*

LEAF MUNCHERS
Yellow poplar weevils have long snouts and their grubs eat tulip tree leaves.

Surprise attack
High up on a branch, the red-tailed hawk watches patiently for signs of food. Its prey includes small mammals and birds. It catches them by surprise, swooping down silently from behind and attacking with its curved claws.

Hanging out
Eastern red bats spend the daytime asleep, hanging from a branch by one leg. As night falls, they fly off to hunt moths and beetles. These bats head south to warmer places before the winter sets in.

A climber's tail
The Virginia opossum normally stays near the ground but it heads up into the trees if it is in danger. Its sharp claws give it a good grip and it can also hang on with its wrap-around prehensile tail.

Maple syrup
In North America, this sweet-tasting sap is collected from sugar maple trees when winter comes to an end. The sap drips through a spout into a bucket tied to the tree.

Cinnamon
This common spice comes from the inner bark of the cinnamon tree, which grows in southeast Asia. After the bark has been peeled off, it curls up into "cinnamon sticks".

Kapok
Kapok seeds are surrounded by fluffy white fibre that is used for filling mattresses and cushions. The fibre must be used carefully because it catches fire easily.

TREASURE FROM
TREES

Trees are some of the most valuable living things on Earth because they can be used in so many different ways. Timber is only one part of this natural harvest. Trees also produce hundreds of different fibres, thousands of oils, resins and dyes, and an almost endless variety of edible fruit and seeds. They yield many substances that we use as medicines, as well as spices that make our food more tasty. And because trees are alive, they can keep on producing year after year. Looked after carefully, trees are a natural treasure chest that never runs out.

~ EYEWITNESS ACCOUNT ~
MY WEDDING DAY

WHERE I LIVE, *in southern India, it is tradition that every bride has the chance to be a work of art! I didn't want to miss out, so my hands and feet were painted with henna, a brown dye that comes from the mignonette tree. Henna takes time to darken, so the painting was done three days before my wedding day. When the big day arrived, the results were fantastic – everyone wanted photos for souvenirs!*

INDIRA SINGH, BRIDE

A work of art

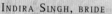
Ground henna

Giant leaves
The raffia palm has the longest leaves of any plant, measuring up to 24 metres (79 ft) from the base of their stalks to their tips. The leaf is divided into narrow leaflets, which stop it from being torn apart by the wind.

1 Raffia leaves are harvested from the wild, where they grow along riverbanks, or from plantations. The men bring them back to the village in large bundles.

RAFFIA FIBRE
Several species of raffia palms are found across tropical Africa, and also in Central and South America. In Madagascar, the Sakalava people use the long leaves as an important fibre crop. The men of the village harvest the leaves and tear them into long strips. These are left to dry in the sun. The women then tie the strips into bundles to be sold.

Raffia products

Raffia is a perfect material for making baskets because it is strong but easy to weave. It is also used for making mats, the soles of beach shoes and garden string. Raffia can be dyed but it is usually left a natural straw colour.

The Kuba people of the Republic of Congo make colourful patterned mats out of raffia. These are used in rituals or even as money.

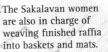

Raffia is used to tie up vegetables such as garlic - a familiar sight in French markets.

2 The tough covering on the underside of the leaf is torn off along its length. Since it is torn rather than cut, the fibres retain their strength.

3 The fibres are left to dry on racks or ropes in the sun, where they eventually turn a pale straw colour. When dry, they are water-resistant and will not shrink.

Raffia is a useful gardening tool. Here, it is being used to graft a tree, a process that involves tying a twig onto a growing tree to support and nourish it.

Tying up raffia into bundles is tiring work.

The Sakalavan women are also in charge of weaving finished raffia into baskets and mats.

4 Some of the finished raffia is used around the village for making ropes and sticks and as building materials, such as supporting beams and roof coverings. The women tie the rest into bundles so it can be sold for export.

Basket weaving is an ancient craft passed on from generation to generation.

Moving timber
In the early days of logging, workers used oxen to drag the timber to the sawmills. These were later replaced by horses, and then by steam power. If logging near a river, rafts of logs could be transported via the water.

LOGGING IN THE PAST
Loggers' lives were tough and lonely. They lived in rough, often lice-infested camps near their worksites, away from their families for months on end. They wore no safety clothing or harnesses, and accidents were common.

Felling
Before the invention of the chainsaw, loggers felled trees using axes or crosscut saws. It took two men to operate these giant saws: one at either end, pushing and pulling in turn. In the above photo the tree is being felled using axes.

TIMBER
HARVESTING

Humans have always used trees, for building, for fuel and for food. However, the practice of forestry – managing trees as a crop, either in natural forests or in plantations – is more recent. This management allows the forester to control the species of tree that is grown, as well as their size, health and quality. Like any other crop, trees can be artificially selected for such things as height or straightness of trunk. And, like any other crop, the trees must eventually be harvested. With today's logging equipment, large areas of forest can be cleared quickly, which makes it vitally important that harvesting is carefully managed.

LOGGING TODAY
Modern machines can grasp a tree, cut it down, remove the bark and side branches, and cut it into lengths in a matter of minutes. A vehicle called a forwarder then carries the stacked logs away to be loaded onto lorries.

~ EYEWITNESS ACCOUNT ~
LOGGER

MY FATHER STARTED *this business 30 years ago, and there's still just the two of us, but with the modern machines we can take down 250 to 400 trees an hour. That's well over 100 tonnes of logs a day, and the machines cut closer to the ground, so you get more timber per tree. But you still have to get out and use your chainsaw from time to time, and that's when it gets dangerous. Trees get hung up on each other and you just don't know which way they're going to drop. Everybody's had a frightening experience at some time.*

ANDY BURKE, TIMBER CUTTER

I wear safety gear and ear protectors while operating a chainsaw.

Replanting seedlings

Aftercare is an important part of forestry. Once trees have been removed, heavy rain can wash away the exposed soil, so it is important to replant. Most modern foresters are required to plant at least one tree for every one they harvest.

Man-made forests

Although timber was originally taken from wild woods, many modern forests are entirely artificial, with trees planted in straight rows. Because they are planted so close together, little can grow beneath them, making them poor habitat for wildlife.

A logging helicopter in action

Helicopter help

In areas where access by road is difficult, such as mountains, timber can be removed by helicopter. This method is better for the environment, as there is no need to build a road to get at the trees.

Christmas cut

In this plantation in southern England, the busiest time of year is December, when 50,000 firs are harvested as Christmas trees. Plantation workers slide special power saws underneath the trees, cutting them just above the ground.

USING
TIMBER

Tens of thousands of years ago, people started using wood as a building material. Today, concrete and steel are used in large buildings but timber still plays a key part in constructing homes. Many houses are built entirely from timber, while others have timber somewhere inside them. That's hardly surprising because wood can be used in so many different ways. It is strong and light, and is also ideal for insulating a house from cold or heat. What's more, wood has a natural beauty that makes it very hard to beat.

Computerised cut
Modern sawmills use computers to minimise waste when a log is cut. After the bark has been stripped off, the log's four sides are cut in turn, producing sets of boards. The strongest wood, at the middle, is used to make timber joists.

Chipboard has the strength needed for upstairs flooring.

WORKING WITH WOOD
The world's oldest timber buildings were made with hardwoods, and each one was a different shape and size. Today, timber-framed houses are made mainly from softwoods, such as pine and spruce, and are often sold as standard kits. A house like this can be ready within weeks – a fraction of the time needed in the past.

WOODLAND CRAFTS

WHEN STONE-AGE farmers began to clear the forests of northern Europe, they discovered that, rather than dying, the felled trees re-sprouted, producing a crop of poles. They could use these poles to make tool handles or to weave hurdles. If left to grow bigger, the poles could be burned to make charcoal. The poles that were not used could be felled later and used for building houses.

POLLARDING *A willow's trunk is cut through above ground level.*

WITHIES *Once the leaves fall, the newly grown withies are ready to be harvested.*

COPPICE POLES *These poles grow straight and are easy to cut and split.*

HURDLES *These woven panels are made from split poles. They were traditionally used for penning sheep.*

From chips to boards
Every year, millions of tonnes of new and waste wood are turned into chips – the first stage in making board. The chips are then coated with glue before being heated and squeezed together. Chipboard is used in furniture and in floors.

TYPES OF WOOD

Plywood can be used to line internal walls.

Roof trusses are often made to measure and then delivered on site.

The timber frame spreads the weight of the house across many joists.

The frame rests on a thin membrane that stops moisture rising upward.

Wood may be pre-treated to prevent insect attack.

External cladding overlaps so that rain runs off without soaking in.

Mahogany is a dense, dark-coloured wood from several species of tropical tree. It is used to make high-quality furniture and musical instruments such as guitars.

Oak is a very strong wood, resistant to attack by insects and fungus, which makes it a good choice for the construction of buildings.

Ebony is a dark, almost black wood used mostly for decorative carving. It is traditionally used for the black keys on a piano.

Walnut is very hard with an attractive grain pattern. It is used to create luxury products such as car interiors.

Cherry is a rich brown wood with a fine grain, making it suitable for carving or turning to produce bowls.

Landscape in wood
Veneers - thin sheets of decorative wood - can be used to create patterns and pictures, a craft known as marquetry.

AN ORCHARDIST'S YEAR
MY ORCHARD

Ripe apples

In some jobs, you do the same work every day. But if you run an organic orchard – like I do – every day is different, so you never have a chance to get bored. Winter is the quietest time but, in spring and summer, I'm often in the orchard until sunset because there's so much to do.

Most of my orchard is taken up with apple trees, although we grow pears and peaches as well. We have several different varieties and we graft each kind onto a dwarf trunk or rootstock, which makes the fruit easier for us to reach. And because the orchard is organic, we don't use any artificial fertilisers or pesticides. Instead, we take extra care to keep the soil in good health and we use natural methods to keep pests at bay. People buy our fruit because they know it is pesticide-free and because it's better for the environment as a whole.

Spring is a crucial time in the orchard because you can't have apples without first having flowers. Once the blossom starts to open, I walk up and down the rows, checking the flowers and making sure that the honeybees are doing their work. Our bees are raised by a local beekeeper and they live in hives placed in gaps among the trees. They are far too busy to worry about us but, even so, we take care not to disturb them close to their hives.

Once the blossom has faded, work shifts up a gear. Every day, I'm on the lookout for curled-up leaves and other signs of insect damage. Although we don't use pesticides, we do use natural insect repellents, such as garlic spray. Speed is vital – if we act quickly, pests have less chance of breeding and getting out of control.

By late spring, I can get an idea of the "set", in other words, how much of the blossom is starting to produce fruit. Surprisingly, we don't want an apple from every flower. If that happened, the trees' branches would split under the weight and the fruit would be much too small to sell. Instead, the ideal set is about one apple for every 20 flowers. If the set is less than this, we can let all the fruit develop. If it's more, we thin out the surplus, giving each apple more room to grow. By early summer, we already have an idea of how good

"...every day is different, so you never have a chance to get bored."

Alternative to multiple grafts

Grafted shoot

Raffia binding

Rootstock

Multiple grafts

Watering the orchard

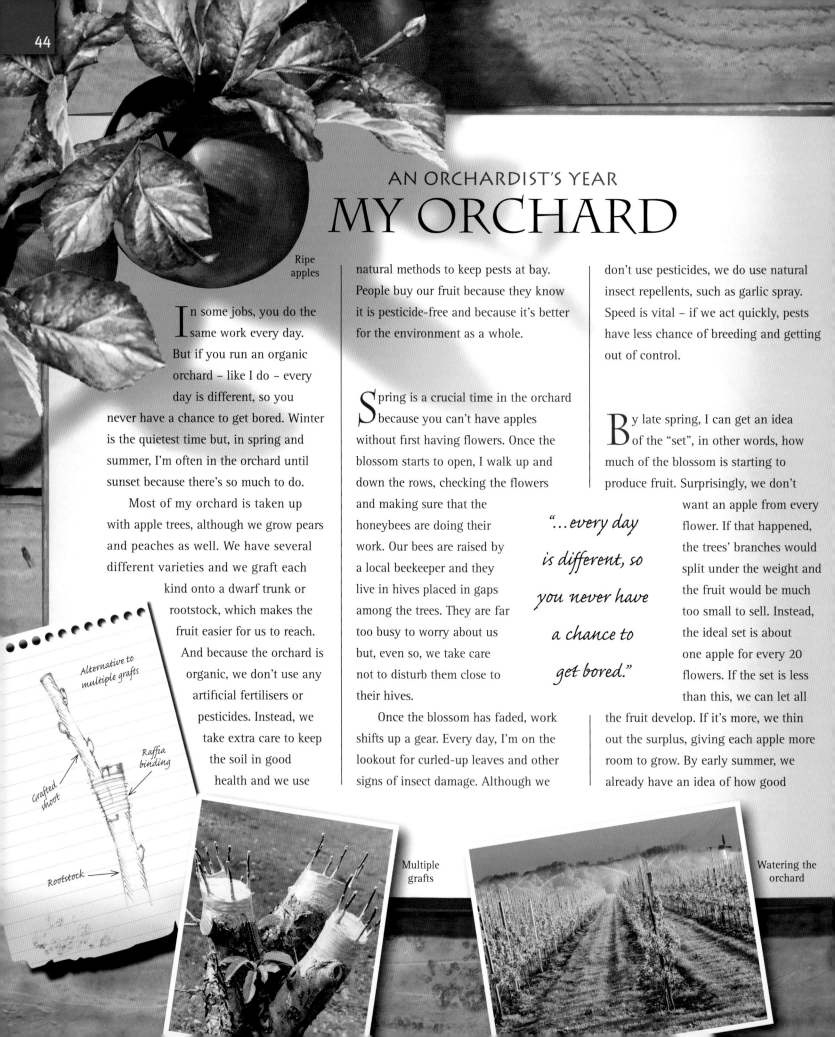

Non-drying glue

Plastic tent

Sticky trap for insect pests

Secateurs

Protective netting

– or bad – the harvest is likely to be.

As the weeks go by, the trees put on a spurt of growth, while the apples swell among the leaves. At this time of year, the fruit makes a tasty target for more insect pests. One of the most troublesome is the codling moth. Its caterpillars bore into the apples, often making them drop from the trees. We keep a careful lookout for any fruit that has fallen early. Although we can't stop the moths from getting into the orchard, we do have some clever ways of fighting back. These include sticky traps that are "baited" with a special scent, called a pheromone. The traps catch the males, which makes it harder for the females to find a mate. Birds can also be a problem, particularly around the edges of the orchard. If they get too pushy, we keep them away from the fruit with nets.

"... what we fear most of all are the thunderstorms because they bring the risk of hail."

With harvest time approaching, good weather becomes more important than ever. If it's hot and dry, we irrigate or water the trees. At this time of the year, what we fear most of all are the thunderstorms because they bring the risk of hail. Hail can destroy an entire crop in minutes and there is no way of knowing where it will strike. Some orchards are protected by hail-proof covers but we try to avoid using plastic, so we cross our fingers and take the risk. As summer comes to an end, the days are usually more settled and the nights start to cool down. It's just what apples need to ripen.

Finally, the big day arrives and we can start the harvest. We pick our apples by hand, using canvas bags to make sure that they don't get bruised.

After that, it's a short tractor ride to the sorting shed, where I keep track of the crop. Because we grow different varieties, our apples ripen at different times. In an average year, the entire harvest can last nearly two months.

Once the last apples are in, we can all take a well-earned rest. Then it's back to work, as the trees gradually lose their leaves. During the winter, we prune the trees and spread compost along the rows so that, by the time spring arrives, we can look forward to an even better harvest than the year before.

Maya Horsnell

Fruit harvest time

Tough leather glove

FORESTS OF THE
WORLD

Forests cover nearly a third of Earth's surface, from the tropics to the edges of the Arctic. Forests vary from place to place because some trees are good at coping with cold or drought, while others need lots of warmth and moisture. There are many ways of classifying forests, depending on where they are, what climate they need or what kind of trees they contain. The map below shows six of the most important forest types. They range in size from the immense boreal forest, in the far north, to temperate rainforest, which is found in only a few parts of the world.

FOREST FRONTIERS

In this map, each type of forest is shown in two different ways. Dark colours show intact forests, where nature is still in control. Pale colours show forests that have been transformed by humans, for example, by being exploited for their timber or partly cleared.

Winter
Conifer trees in the boreal forest can survive the snowy months. Their leaves, or needles, are undamaged by frost and stay on the tree all year long. These needles, which are thick and waxy to resist the cold, also shed heavy coverings of snow easily.

BOREAL FOREST

Also known as the taiga, this is the world's biggest forest, stretching almost all the way around the far north of the globe. The name "boreal" comes from Boreas, the Greek god of the north wind, and hints at the forest's climate – long, harsh winters and short, moist summers. The forest contains mainly conifers, mixed with broadleaved trees that can cope with the intense winter cold.

KEY
MAJOR FORESTS

BOREAL
INTACT FOREST
NO LONGER INTACT

TEMPERATE CONIFEROUS
INTACT FOREST
NO LONGER INTACT

TEMPERATE BROADLEAF
INTACT FOREST
NO LONGER INTACT

TEMPERATE RAINFOREST
INTACT FOREST
NO LONGER INTACT

TROPICAL RAINFOREST
INTACT FOREST
NO LONGER INTACT

TROPICAL SEASONAL
INTACT FOREST
NO LONGER INTACT

North America · Europe · Asia · Africa · South America · Australia · Equator

BOREAL FOREST

Forest type: Evergreen
Major areas: North America, Scandinavia, northern Asia
Max. temperature: 30°C (86°F)
Min. temperature: −50°C (−58°F)
Typical rainfall: 500 millimetres (20 in)

Clever bill

Crossbills are perfectly designed for life in the boreal forest. With the forest's large number of spruce and pine trees, they rarely want for food. A crossbill's unusual crossed bill allows it to rip cone scales apart and extract the tasty seed inside with its tongue.

Canadian forest

The boreal forest in Canada forms a band around 1,000 kilometres (621 miles) wide and makes up 35 per cent of the whole country's land. It is home to many types of wildlife including the elk, a type of deer. Males of this species have large antlers and a thick mane. Grey wolves also live in the forest, hunting in packs for their favourite food – deer.

Originally from Scotland, the Scots pine has a long straight trunk with needles that grow in pairs and egg-shaped cones.

Native to Japan, the Japanese umbrella pine has short branches arranged in circles around the trunk. Its leaves are scale like.

The North American white oak has leaves with a jagged outline and light, cup-shaped acorns.

The trunk of the New Zealand soft tree fern supports a crown of beautiful green fronds.

Growing on trees

In wet forests, many plants grow in trees to reach the light. Plants like this are called epiphytes. This epiphytic moss is growing on a tree in temperate rainforest. It gets all the moisture it needs from rain.

BOREAL

Boreal forest, Siberia

Temperate coniferous forest, Japan

TEMPERATE

Temperate broadleaf forest, USA

Temperate rainforest, New Zealand

Tropical rainforest, Borneo

TROPICAL

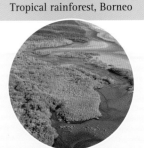

Tropical seasonal forest, Costa Rica

Manioc
The bushy manioc plant (also known as cassava) is a staple food of the Huaorani people. They boil the root as a vegetable, or grind it to make flour.

FOREST
DWELLERS

For thousands of years, people have made their homes in forests. Prehistoric hunter-gatherers found ample food in forests and woodlands, and knew which plants were poisonous and which could be used as medicine. Today, people still live in rainforests in some parts of the world. Traditionally they have lived in harmony with their forest home. However, these indigenous communities are under threat from over-harvesting of their trees and diseases introduced by new settlers.

BAMBUTI PEOPLE

Also called the Mbuti, these people live in the Ituri rainforest in the Democratic Republic of Congo. They are pygmies, and adult males grow only to 150 centimetres (4 ft 11 in). The men hunt forest animals, while the women gather fruits and plants.

HUAORANI PEOPLE

These people live in the Amazon rainforest of Ecuador. They hunt with blowguns which have darts made from the toxic curare vine. They believe that this is a humane way to kill animals.

Forest camps
The Bambuti are nomadic – they move around the forest and set up camps. This lifestyle is less damaging to the rainforest as they don't over-strip any area of life or growth. Their huts are made from saplings and leaves.

NORTHERN FOREST DWELLERS

Sami people have lived in the northern boreal forest for more than 2,000 years. This cold environment, which runs through parts of northern Norway, Sweden, Finland and Russia, is very different from the hot and humid rainforests of Africa and South America. The Sami still live mostly on food found in the forest, including reindeer, berries and fish.

Aztec mask
The Aztecs were skilled craftworkers and made beautiful objects from precious stones such as turquoise and jade. This jade mask was probably used in religious ceremonies.

Teeth were made out of bone.

Aztecs considered jade to be more valuable than gold.

ANCIENT DWELLERS

Hundreds of years ago, several great civilisations flourished in and around the rainforests of Mexico, Central America and the Andes. These were the Maya, from Central America and Mexico; the Aztecs, from Mexico; and the Inca, from the Andes in South America. Their people lived in complex societies, built cities and farmed the land.

PAPUAN PEOPLE

The people who made these remote jungle homes in the forested highlands of western New Guinea have little contact with the outside world. Their way of life has remained virtually unchanged for centuries because it is so difficult for outsiders to reach the traditional forest villages.

Mayan home
The Maya of today live in homes similar to those built by their ancestors. The walls have woven sticks covered with soil, weeds and water. The roofs are thatched with reeds and grasses.

FORESTS UNDER THREAT

Forests around the world are in grave danger for many reasons.

Indonesia's forests up in smoke

The thick cloud of smoke in the skies above the city of Pontianak, Borneo, has become a familiar sight in recent years. The smoke comes from hundreds of brush, forest and peat fires burning across Sumatra and Borneo.

Most are thought to have been started deliberately as a cheap and quick way to clear land, and the result is widespread misery as air quality drops to dangerous levels. More worrying for the long term, however, is the loss of the forests themselves. Since 1990, an estimated 28.1 million hectares (69.4 mill ac) of forest have been destroyed. Of that total, 7.2 million hectares (17.8 mill ac) were primary forest – unspoilt jungle that had never been cleared for logging and was rich in wildlife. This year's fires were made worse by El Niño, the 3–8 year variation in the climate of the tropical Pacific, which had caused a recent lengthy drought.

Wildlife in danger

Species threatened by the continued loss of primary rainforest include the orangutan, which is being driven out of its natural habitat into nearby plantations. Here, the great apes come into conflict with farmers, who kill them as pests. But orangutans are only one of the more visible species to be affected. Many insects, reptiles and birds are also being driven to extinction

Smoke rises from runaway forest fires, outside Pekanbaru, Indonesia.

Hurricane Felix disaster

Wild winds destroy irreplaceable rainforest.

A recent Rainforest Alliance study of Nicaragua's forests found that 2007's Hurricane Felix devastated nearly 1 million hectares (2.5 mill ac) of forest in the north of the country. Felix, a category 5 hurricane, hit Nicaragua after passing through the Caribbean, where it caused widespread damage to property.

hurricane, but on 4 September it increased in strength once more and tore into the coast of Nicaragua with winds up to 257 kilometres per hour (160 mph). Around 130 people died as a result, but luckily in Nicaragua it avoided major centres of population. The damage to the country's forests,

Grey squirrels wreak havoc

Alien invader drives out native squirrels and destroys woodlands.

They may seem cute, with their tufted ears and bushy tails, but in the world of squirrels, a secret war is being fought. The familiar grey squirrel, it turns out, is not native to the UK, but is in fact an alien invader, imported from North America. And it is out-competing the native red squirrel, which is now on the endangered list. The larger, stronger grey squirrel has the advantage over its red cousin when it comes to finding food, and can also store fat more effectively in winter. But this ability to thrive in the UK comes at another price. The grey squirrel is not only killing off its relatives, it is destroying the very woodlands it depends upon, by stripping the bark from trees.

Spider monkey on way out!

Pushed to the brink of extinction by forest destruction

The seven species of spider monkey found in South America are facing extinction as a result of the destruction of their forest habitat. Illegal logging, road construction and clearance for agriculture have resulted in a drastic decline in population numbers, with one species – the black-headed spider monkey – now close to the brink of extinction. This is bad news not only for the monkeys themselves but for the forest as a whole – the monkeys play a vital role in dispersing the seeds of many forest plants.

Acid rain – an ecological disaster

Western Europe to lose 48 million cubic metres (157 mill cu ft) of timber a year

Forests may be at more risk from acid rain than scientists previously thought. It was believed that the main effect on trees came from the acidity of the rainwater directly affecting the leaves. However, recent research shows that the rain may actually be washing vital nutrients out of the soil. The increased acidity – caused by industrial pollution and car exhausts – dissolves chemicals such as magnesium and calcium in the forest soils, allowing these chemicals to be washed away. And without them, more sensitive tree species become weakened and die in harsh winters.

Although the phenomenon of acid rain was first noted in the lakes of Scandinavia, the great pine forests of Germany were next to suffer. By 1986 around 54 per cent of the total forest area, about 4 million hectares (9.9 mill ac), was affected, with trees either sick or dying. And the trend continues – acid rain will continue to devastate forests unless countries cooperate to prevent it.

Dead spruce trees killed by acid rain, Karkonosze National Park, Poland

Amazon "green gold" racket finally exposed

As much as 80 per cent of tropical timber felled illegally

Known as "green gold", the wood of the mahogany tree has been used for centuries to construct the finest furniture. Every tree is therefore very valuable. But as much as 80 per cent of the mahogany exported to the USA and Europe may be from illegal sources, claims a report by the Natural Resources Commission. Because of their long history of exploitation, mahogany trees are becoming increasingly rare in the wild and are protected by law. However, recent aerial photographs show that mahogany continues to be felled from large areas of pristine Amazonian rainforest.

Illegal loggers with a shipment of rainforest timber

Fatal disease takes hold

Thousands of trees lost to deadly disease

Thousands of elm trees across Britain are dying as a result of a disease brought into the country in a shipment of timber. Dutch elm disease – so-called because it was first identified in Holland – is a fungal disease spread from tree to tree by bark beetles. A mild strain of the disease arrived in the country in 1927, but had largely died out by 1940. However, a much more vigorous strain was imported from North America in 1967, in a shipment of logs. This strain spread rapidly, and today very few mature elms remain.

The tunnels caused by the elm bark beetle

TREE MYTHS AND
LEGENDS

Deer fed on Yggdrasil's leaves.

Holly has shiny green leaves and bright red berries.

Mysterious thorny forests feature in many folk stories and fairytales. With their roots reaching deep into the ground and their branches soaring towards the heavens, trees seem to link our Earth with other, unseen worlds. Moreover, many trees have a cycle of growth, decay and rebirth, which links them to ancient myths and religious beliefs.

YGGDRASIL
In Viking mythology, Yggdrasil, or the world tree, was an ash tree that grew on an island. Its roots delved into the underworld, while its branches reached up to the skies, spreading out over all the countries in the world. It provided nourishment for gods, humans and animals.

WINTER EVERGREENS
For centuries, evergreen trees such as holly and fir have been seen as symbols of life in the cold and darkness of winter. Holly leaves brought into the house were said to ward off evil fairies. Decorating Christmas trees dates back to the ancient Romans, who adorned fir trees with bits of metal around the feast of Saturnalia (17 December).

Christmas tree
Today, people decorate fir trees at Christmas, often placing brightly wrapped presents underneath.

Hebe's magical chalice was filled with youth-giving ambrosia.

Rowan leaves are shaped like an eagle's feathers; the berries are like drops of blood.

DRYADS
A dryad is a tree nymph (female spirit) from Greek mythology. Dryads were strongly tied to their tree-homes (usually an oak). If the tree were harmed, the dryad would perish too. Anyone guilty of this deed was punished by the gods.

THE ROWAN
The hardy rowan tree's mythical story begins in ancient Greece. When Hebe, the goddess of youth, lost her chalice to demons, the gods sent an eagle to retrieve it. The fight that ensued caused feathers and blood to fall on the earth; each grew into a rowan tree.

Dryads usually lived in oak trees.

TREES IN THE BIBLE

Trees are used as symbols in the Bible. The tree of knowledge of good and evil grew in the Garden of Eden. God had forbidden Adam and Eve to eat its fruit, but they were tempted by a serpent and tasted the fruit. Their punishment was to be denied access to the tree of life – meaning immortality – and death has ever since been the fate of humans.

To·him·that·overcometh·will·I·give to·eat·of·the·tree·of·life·which·is·in the·midst·of·the·Paradise·of·God

The tree of life promised eternal life

YEW TREES

Since pre-Christian times, yew trees have been considered sacred – possibly because they can live for up to 3,000 years. The Celts planted them in sacred sites and, when Christianity arrived, churches were often built on these sites. To this day, yew trees stand in many churchyards and cemeteries.

Yew needles are extremely poisonous.

Yew wood was used to make longbows in medieval times.

The peepal tree has heart-shaped leaves and bears a purple fruit.

HINDU TREE

The peepal tree, also known as the sacred fig or Asvattha tree, is native to India and is revered by Hindus. It grows with its roots in the spirit world and its branches in the visible world. Cutting or harming the peepal tree in any way is considered a sin.

TREES IN LITERATURE

TREES HAVE INSPIRED authors and poets alike. C.S. Lewis created a forest of talking trees in his *Chronicles of Narnia*. His Tree of Protection, grown from the Tree of Youth, guarded the country of Narnia from evil for 900 years. Lewis's friend, J.R.R. Tolkein, populated his magical world of Middle Earth in *Lord of the Rings* with humanised trees called ents.

THE WHITE WITCH *The evil witch Jadis seized power in Narnia and turned the land into an endless winter. She used tree spirits as her spies and allies.*

TREEBEARD *The character called Treebeard was the oldest of all ents. He lived in the mythical Forest of Fangorn, and stood tall and straight like a tree.*

TREE
FACTS

Read on to learn some fascinating facts about trees - from the record breakers to those that are just truly amazing.

The world's oldest tree
Somewhere in California's White Mountains, a bristlecone pine named Methuselah has been growing for more than 4,800 years. It's the world's oldest living thing – but its location is a closely guarded secret.

PREHISTORIC TREES

THE WORLD'S TREES include some remarkable survivors from the distant past. The ginkgo, a unique tree with no living relatives, was saved from extinction by monks in China. The Wollemi pine has an even stranger history. It survived in secret, in the Blue Mountains of eastern Australia. It was discovered by a park ranger in 1994.

TRAPPED IN AMBER *This grasshopper became caught in tree resin millions of years ago. The resin fossilised and turned into amber.*

GINKGO *After its brush with extinction, the ginkgo has now become a common city tree.*

WOLLEMI PINE
Fewer than a hundred adult Wollemi pines exist in the wild.

LIGHTEST WOOD

THE BALSA TREE, from South America, has the lightest wood in the world. On average, it weighs only a third as much as the wood from other broadleaved trees. It is seven times less dense than water, which means that it floats even better than cork. Despite being light, balsa wood is remarkably strong. It is used for making models, surfboards and ocean-going rafts. In the past, it was even used in fighter planes.

HIDDEN HOLES
Balsa wood contains millions of air-filled spaces, which make it unusually light.

EPIC VOYAGE
In 1947, the explorer Thor Heyerdahl crossed the Pacific Ocean on a balsa-wood raft.

HEAVIEST SEED

THE WORLD'S LARGEST and heaviest seeds are produced by the coco de mer palm, which grows in the remote Seychelles Islands in the Indian Ocean. The seeds look like two coconuts joined together. They measure up to 90 centimetres (3 ft) in circumference and can weigh 20 kilograms (44 lb). Coco de mer palms are either male or female. The female trees produce just a handful of nuts each year.

DOUBLE NUT *A local ranger holds up a coco de mer nut. Unlike a true coconut, this nut cannot float.*

MOST SWOLLEN TRUNK

ACCORDING TO an old African tradition, the baobab is planted upside down, with its roots in the air. This extraordinary tree has short, thick branches and a swollen trunk that works like a living reservoir. Big baobabs can hold more than 100,000 litres (22,000 gal) of water, which helps them to survive long droughts. Elephants sometimes gouge the trunk with their tusks when they need a drink.

WATER TANK
Baobabs grow in Africa, Madagascar and Australia. Some can be more than a thousand years old.

~ FIND OUT MORE ~
SEARCHING THE WEB

www.globaltrees.org
Focuses on saving threatened tree species. Lists endangered trees and conservation projects.

www.kids.mongabay.com
Contains information on tropical rainforests - their trees, animals and people.

www.rainforest-alliance.org/education
Packed with fun facts about the rainforest, stories, and hands-on projects to do.

www.pbs.org/journeyintoamazonia
Includes information on the PBS wildlife series about Amazonia - its plants, life in the canopy and conservation issues.

www.mbgnet.net/sets/taiga
Focuses on the taiga habitat, with lots of information on its plants, animals and climate.

www.mbgnet.net/sets/temp
Contains lots of information on the temperate deciduous habitat - its seasons, leaves and forest animals.

DID YOU KNOW?

In California, a giant sequoia called General Sherman has an estimated weight of at least 5,500 tonnes (5,400 t). It is about 2,500 years old.

The trunk of the boojum tree, from northern Mexico, is a snakelike pole. It can grow up to 20 metres (65 ft) high but its branches are often just pencil sized.

The dwarf willow can be more than 1 metre (3 ft) across, but just 5 centimetres (2 in) high. It lives in the Arctic and on mountains further south.

A sacred fig tree was planted in Anuradhapura, Sri Lanka, about 2,300 years ago. The world's oldest known planted tree is still alive and well.

The roots of a wild South African fig tree have been found in a cave, 120 metres (390 ft) underground. This is the greatest known depth for tree roots.

The durian tree, from Southeast Asia, grows large fruit with a very powerful odour. Some people can smell it from more than 50 metres (165 ft) away.

The sugar pine, a conifer that grows in the western United States, has the longest cones. They can grow up to 60 centimetres (24 in) long.

Until 2003, there was just one café marron tree in the world. Scientists have now managed to grow more from cuttings, to stop it becoming extinct.

Rattan palms, from Southeast Asia, can be up to 200 metres (656 ft) long. Instead of standing up straight, they sprawl through other trees.

The lignum vitae has some of the densest wood, which is so heavy that it cannot float. The tree grows in Central America and the Caribbean.

Greatest girth
A Montezuma cypress in Oaxaca, Mexico, has the thickest single trunk, measuring about 35 metres (114 ft) in circumference. A baobab in South Africa measures 47 metres (154 ft) but it divides in two close to the ground.

GLOSSARY

ALTERNATE LEAVES Leaves that grow singly, alternating between different sides of a stem or twig.

ANGIOSPERM The scientific name for plants that grow flowers. Angiosperms include almost all of the world's trees, apart from conifers.

ANTHERS The parts of flowers that produce pollen. Anthers open when their pollen is ripe.

AXIL The angle between a leaf stalk and a twig or between one twig and another.

BARK The tough outer skin of a tree, which protects its wood from damage. Unlike wood, the outer part of bark is dead.

BEDROCK Solid rock buried beneath the surface of the ground. Bedrock slowly releases chemical nutrients into the soil, enabling plants to grow.

BOREAL FOREST The forest that stretches around the far north, on the fringes of the Arctic. Also known as taiga, it is made up mainly of coniferous trees.

BROADLEAVED TREE A tree that has flat, wide leaves and that reproduces by growing flowers. There are thousands of species of broadleaved trees, which grow all over the world.

BUD A tiny shoot that is protected by tough scales. The bud bursts open when the shoot starts to grow.

BUTTRESS ROOTS Roots that reach upward, as supports to brace a tree's trunk. Buttress roots are common in rainforest trees.

CAMBIUM A thin sheet of highly active cells, just beneath a tree's bark. The cells in the cambium keep dividing to make new bark and new wood. See also MERISTEM.

CARBON DIOXIDE A gas in the atmosphere that all plants need to grow. They collect it from the air with their leaves.

CARPELS The female parts of a flower. Carpels collect pollen, so that a flower can make seeds.

CELLS The microscopic building blocks of all living things. Trees contain hundreds of millions of cells, in many different sizes and shapes. Together, they carry out the different tasks needed for a tree to grow.

CHLOROPHYLL The green substance that trees and other plants use to collect the energy in sunlight.

CHLOROPLASTS Tiny green structures that contain chlorophyll. Chloroplasts are found mainly in leaves. They harness solar energy and turn it into chemical energy that the plant can use.

COMPOUND LEAF A leaf that is made of separate parts, known as leaflets.

CONIFER A tree with narrow or scale-shaped leaves, which makes seeds in cones. Unlike broadleaved trees, conifers do not have flowers.

DECIDUOUS TREE A tree that loses all of its leaves for part of the year.

DEFORESTATION The destruction of forests by people. Once deforestation has ocurred, it is often permanent.

DICOT A flowering plant that has two special leaves pre-packed inside its seeds. Most broadleaved trees belong to this group of plants.

EMBRYONIC Something that is at a very early stage of development.

ENDODERMIS An inner layer in roots; cells in this layer control the movement of substances in the roots.

EPIDERMIS An outer layer in roots; cells in this layer often have microscopic root hairs that absorb water from the soil.

EPIPHYTE A plant (usually a vine) that grows on a tree, without harming it.

EVERGREEN TREE A tree that keeps its leaves all year round.

FRUIT In flowering plants, the parts that contain seeds and help them to spread. Broadleaved trees have many different kinds of fruits – some are soft, but others are hard and dry.

GERMINATION The moment when a seed starts to grow.

GLUCOSE An energy-rich sugar used by plants and most other living things. Animals get glucose from their food but plants make it themselves, by carrying out photosynthesis.

GRAFT Fastening the cut stem of one tree onto the roots of another. Once a tree has been grafted, the stem and roots slowly join together.

GROWTH RINGS Rings in wood, produced by yearly layers of growth. Counting these rings tells you the age of a tree.

GYMNOSPERM A plant that makes seeds without growing flowers. The most common gymnosperms are conifers.

Dipterocarp seeds

HABITAT The surroundings that a plant or animal needs to survive.

HARDWOOD The wood of broadleaved trees, apart from palms.

HEARTWOOD A tree's oldest and hardest wood, in the very centre of its trunk.

HIBERNATING Spending the winter in a deep "sleep". When mammals hibernate, their body temperature drops until they are almost as cold as their surroundings.

HUMUS A fertile mixture of soil and the remains of rotted wood and leaves.

LEAF LITTER The layer of dead leaves on the ground in a woodland or forest.

LENTICELS Spongy pores on bark or fruit, which connect a tree's living cells with the air.

Date palm

Yew

Mignonette

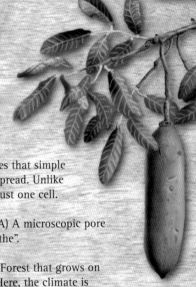

Sausage tree

ERISTEM Any part of a plant where cells ...ide rapidly, making the plant grow. Trees ...ve meristems at the tips of their stems and ...ots, and also beneath their bark.

IGRATING Travelling between two different ...rts of the world at particular times of the year.

ONOCOT A flowering plant that has a single ...f pre-packed inside its seeds. Monocot trees ...clude all palm trees.

YCORRHIZAE Living partnerships between ...ots and soil-dwelling fungi. Fungi are good at ...llecting nutrients, so these partnerships help ...ants to grow.

UTRIENT A substance that living things need ... grow. Compared to animals, plants need very ...mple nutrients, which they get from the air or ...m the soil.

PPOSITE LEAVES Leaves that are attached ... the stem in pairs.

VARY The part of a flower that contains the ...veloping seeds. When an ovary ripens, it forms ...rt of a fruit.

VULES A flower's female cells, which have to ... pollinated before they can turn into seeds.

XYGEN One of the most important gases in the ...mosphere. Animals take in oxygen when they ...eathe. Plants release oxygen back into the air ...en they carry out photosynthesis.

AT A crumbly substance made from the partly ...cayed remains of plants.

HEROMONES Special scents that animals use ... signal to other members of their species.

PHLOEM A system of cells that plants use to move sap and the substances that it contains.

PHOTOSYNTHESIS A way of using sunlight to grow. Photosynthesis is carried out by all

green plants – including trees – and some kinds of bacteria.

POLLEN Dust-like grains that contain the male cells of a flower.

POLLINATION The movement of pollen from flower to flower, so that seeds can be made.

POLLUTION Anything that harms living things by contaminating land, water or air.

PREDATOR An animal that hunts and catches other animals for food.

PROP ROOTS Roots that arch outward from a tree's trunk, helping to prop it up in soft ground.

RAINFOREST A forest that grows where the climate is always wet. Most of the world's rainforests are in the tropics but some rainforests grow in colder parts of the world.

RESIN A sticky substance that some trees use to protect themselves. Resin is most common in conifers.

ROOT CAP A cap of slippery cells on the tip of a root, which protects the root and helps it to push through the soil.

ROOT HAIRS Microscopic hairs near the tip of a root, which absorb moisture and nutrients from the soil.

ROOTSTOCK A small stump with roots, which is used when grafting a tree.

SAP The watery fluid that moves up and down trees. It contains sugars and many other dissolved substances.

SAPWOOD Newly grown wood near the outside of a tree's trunk.

SEEDS Tough packages of living cells that most trees use to reproduce. Each one contains a tiny embryo plant and built-in food supply.

SHOOT The above-ground part of any plant.

SIMPLE LEAF A leaf that has a single and undivided blade.

SOFTWOOD The wood of coniferous trees, such as spruces and pines.

SPORES Dust-like particles that simple plants, like ferns, use to spread. Unlike seeds, spores often have just one cell.

STOMA (plural STOMATA) A microscopic pore that a plant uses to "breathe".

SUBTROPICAL FOREST Forest that grows on the edges of the tropics. Here, the climate is often split into a wet season and a dry season.

TAIGA Another name for boreal forest.

TEMPERATE FOREST Forest that grows in the world's temperate regions, between the tropics and the poles. Here, summers can be warm but winters are often long and cold.

THYLAKOID A disc-like sac that contains chlorophyll. Thylakoids are stacked up inside chloroplasts and they play a key part in collecting the energy in sunshine.

TOPSOIL The topmost part of the soil; trees get most of their nutrients from this layer.

TRANSPIRATION Movement of water from the soil, up a tree and out through its leaves.

TROPICAL FOREST Forest that grows on or near the Equator. Most tropical forests are evergreen because the climate is good for growing all year round.

TUNDRA A cold treeless habitat that is found in the far north and on high mountains.

WHORLED LEAVES Leaves that are attached in circles around a stem or twig.

XYLEM A system of cells that plants use to move water. Xylem stretches from the tips of a plant's roots to all of its leaves.

Cycad

Dipterocarp

INDEX

CREDITS

The publisher thanks Steve Alton, Caroline Buckingham, Christopher Davies, Christina McInerney, Susan McKeever, Andrea Pinnington and Corinne Roberts for their contributions and Jo Rudd for the index.

Key t=top; l=left; r=right; tl=top left; tcl=top center left; tc=top center; tcr=top center right; tr=top right; cl=center left; c=center; cr=center right; b=bottom; bl=bottom left; bcl=bottom center left; bc=bottom center; bcr=bottom center right; br=bottom right

ILLUSTRATIONS

Peter Bull Art Studio Cover, 4tl, 5tr, 6–7, 8–13, 14–15, 16–17, 18–19, 20–21, 22–5, 26–7, 28–9, 39, 42–3, 56–7; James McKinnon 5tl, 46–51; Yvan Meunier/Contact Jupiter 4tr, 32–3, 34–7; Roger Stewart/KJA-artists 30–1, 44–5
Maps by Andrew Davies/Creative Communication
Pop up taxonomy by Peter Bull Art Studio
Graphic novel by Rob Davis and Geraint Ford/The Art Agency

PHOTOGRAPHS

ALA = Alamy, BM = British Museum, CBT = Corbis Traditional Licensing, GI = Getty Images, IS = istockphoto.com, MP = Minden Pictures, NGS = National Geographic Society, NHPA = NHPA, PG = Pavel German, PS = Photoshot, SH = Shutterstock, TPL = Photolibrary.com, Wiki = Public Domain

1c, cc iS; 3c GI; tc iS; 4b, c iS; 6bc, bc, bc, bc, c, c, cc, cl, cl SH; 7br, br, cr iS; br SH; 8tc, tr GI; tr iS; cl PG; 9tl TPL; 12tl iS; TPL; 13c, cc, cl TPL; 14br GI; tr iS; tl, tl, tr SH; tc, tc, tl TPL; 15bc GI; tc, tr, tr iS; tl, tl TPL; 16cr TPL; 17bc GI; tr iS; bc, bl, br, er, cr, tr, tr TPL; 19br iS; br wiki; 21bc iS; bc, tc TPL; 22br, tc TPL; 23bl, cl, cl, tl TPL; 24bc TPL; 25c, t, t, t iS; b, c, c TPL 26c GI; br, br iS; bc, bc, bl, cc, cl, cl, cr SH; 27bc, bc, bc, bc, br TPL; 28c, tl iS; cl, tl TPL; 29c, cc iS; tr NHPA; 30bc CBT; bl iS; 31bc, tr iS; bc TPL; 32bc, c, cc, cl, cl TPL; 33tr iS; c, cr TPL; 34bl iS; bl TPL; 35tc ALA; bc SH; bc, bl, tl TPL; 36tl ALA; 38cl CBT; bl GI; bc iS; cr PS; tl SH; bl, tr TPL; 39bc CBT; br, c, cr, tr, tr iS; 40bl, tl TPL; br, cl-iS; br TPL; 41bl, br GI; br iS; t, tr TPL 42bl, tl iS; bc, bl, cl, cl TPL; 43br ALA; cr GI; br iS; cr, tr SH; cr TPL; 44br iS; bc TPL; 45bc, br iS; tc TPL; 46br SH; 47tl iS; tr TPL; 49c, cc, tc iS; bc, tl SH; cl TPL; 51tl ALA; tc GI; bc, bc, tl iS; br MP; cr, cr, tr, tr SH; b, c, cr TPL; 52br, cr ALA; bl, tl PS; 53tr BM; bc, t GI; br, cr iS; 56br, br, c, cl, cr, cr, t, tc, tl iS; br, tl TPL; 57bc CBT; b, bc, bc, bc, bc, br, br, c, cc, cr, cr, cr, tr iS; SH; tl TPL; 58bc, cl, tl iS; bc, cl SH; bl TPL; 59br CBT; br, c, t, tr iS; cl NGS; bl, cr, tl TPL; 61b, c, t, t, t iS; b, t, t TPL

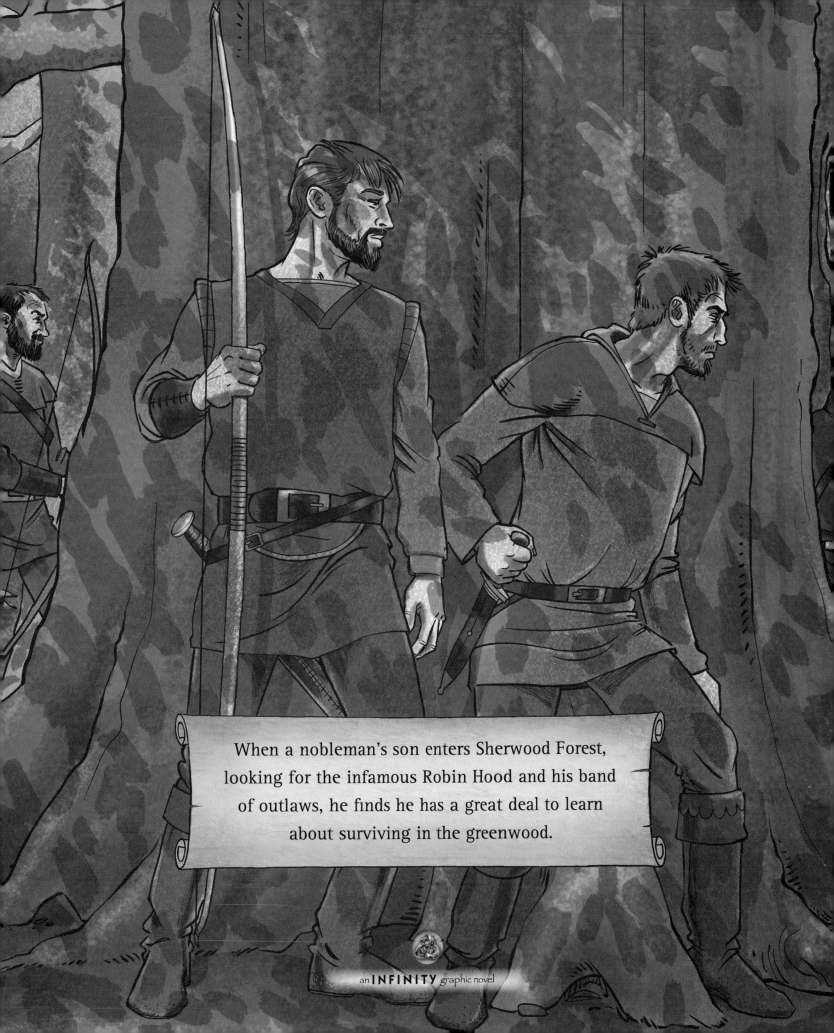

When a nobleman's son enters Sherwood Forest,
looking for the infamous Robin Hood and his band
of outlaws, he finds he has a great deal to learn
about surviving in the greenwood.

an **INFINITY** graphic novel

An Adventure in
SHERWOOD FOREST

Based on the Legend
of
Robin Hood

INFINITY